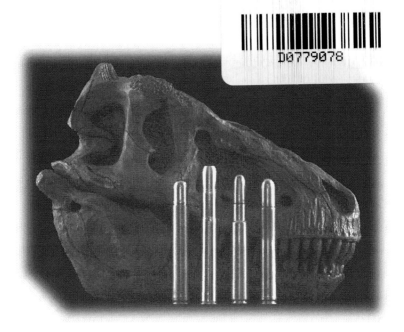

rexGun

by Dr. Stephen W. Templar

ISBN 978-0-615-22413-8

Ivory Lady Publishing
Winchester, Virginia

Printed In The
United States of America

www.rexGun.com

rexGun@rexGun.com

Dedication

Dedicated to my wife:
Morgan Anne Templar

And, to my old friend and
gun bearer, Tiek, who stood
steadfast by my side as we
faced some terrifying beasts

Acknowledgements

I wish to acknowledge those people who have helped make the completion of this book possible. It is their inspiration, advice, patience and examples that have aided me in the completion of my work.

Morgan A. Templar
Autumn, Subrina, Dale and Robert - my children
Arthur Alphin
Tiffany & Robert Hall
Lori & Todd "Sasquasher" Grimmett
Gregor Woods
Bradley K. Kendall
James L. Smith
William "Bulletforge" Preston
Butch Searcy
Todd A. Hanson
Peggy & Walter Keller
Layfe "505" Anthony, MD
Don Heath
Kent "Cory" Cannon
P. H. Capstick
S. Ping & B. Chu
E. A. "Sylvrin" Tiek & Lizzie

Table of Contents

Introduction -------------------------------- 9

Part 1: Predator rex --------------------- 11

Part 2: Terminal Medicine --------------- 27

Part 3: Laws and Formulae ------------- 67

Laws of Ballistic Dynamics ---------------- 71

Bullet Impact Zone (BIZ) ------------------ 72

Terminal Medicine (T.Rx) ------------------ 77

T.Rx Formula ------------------------------ 86

Part 4: Tables & Errata ----------------- 87

Table-1: rexGun Cartridges ---------------- 89

Table-2: Species Specific T.Rx Values ----- 96

Table-3: Terminal Effect. Comparison ----- 97

Table-4: Weight to T.Rx -------------------- 98

Introduction

In my younger days I recall observing a fully fleshed out *Tyrannosaurus rex* mount in one of my favorite museums. One could view the beast from many angles and from multiple levels.

I spent countless hours looking upon that *T. rex* and asking myself: Where, in that monstrous predator, would I put the bullet if I were hunting such a creature? And, what sort of bullet would it need to be?

After all, this beast was unlike any I had ever hunted or even seen; fleshed out, its appearance, design and scale seemed completely foreign to me.

Somehow these questions, this situation, felt very real. Much time would pass before I discovered why.

To most people, even hunters, the question of proper weapon selection for the sporting pursuit of *Tyrannosaurus rex* seems, at first glance, to be something of a moot issue. However, it is not...

Part 1: Predator rex

Let go of the Saturday matinee images of the *Tyrannosaurus rex* and start watching Stephen Spielberg's *Jurassic Park* movies over and over again. Even those tyrannosaurs are a bit small for *T. rex*. Check the measurements, do your homework and you will find that *T. rex* are big, really big... bigger than big.

Of utmost importance is that you, the hunter, realize that *Tyrannosaurus rex* are not giant iguanas standing on their hind legs in a vain attempt to look menacing. *T. rex* are colossal, fast, agile super-predators with more power at their disposal than can be fully comprehended. They have the weapons and cunning of a predator, the vicious contempt of a scavenger and they are truly menacing.

There are no second chances with this monster.

Old-Style Tyrannosaurus rex

You cannot hope to shoot this predator out of the air, like a leaping leopard. Nor can you hope to survive the initial strike long enough for your backup to save you, as with the African lion. You cannot hope to jump aside at the last moment as you might with a charging rhinoceros. The leg bones of a large *T. rex*, while hollow, make the shoulder bones of elephants seem insignificant by comparison. In fact, *Tyrannosaurus rex* are so large, so massive, that there is almost no chance at all of even disabling one by shooting out one of its hips, knees or ankles with anything less than a true Elephant Rifle, something like a 470 Nitro Express. Don't be fooled, even with such a weapon the odds of crippling one in that way are not great.

This is why the selection of a rifle for use in the sporting pursuit of *Tyrannosaurus rex*, a rexGun, is so deserving of thoughtful assessment and requires such careful consideration. The question of how much gun is truly enough to provide a reasonable chance of success against a *T. rex* is critically important; your life, and the lives of those in your hunting party, may very well depend upon it.

As when choosing most hunting firearms, the selection of a rexGun is largely a matter of taste and is secondary to the skill level of the hunter.

When hunting dangerous game, adequate shot placement and the ability to make quick and accurate follow-up shots are of the utmost importance. That said, when hunting tyrannosaurs the reliability and effectiveness of the firearm and load to be used are even more important because of the scale of the predator.

Still, be mindful that a super-powered weapon is useless if it cannot be brought to bear exactly when, where and as quickly as it is needed. Consider that the larger and more dangerous the prey is, the less room for error there is in weapon selection and training; tyrannosaurs are extremely large and well beyond dangerous.

Just as excellent marksmen have used rifles as small as 6.5mm to take African elephant, a lighter rifle than those I recommend in this book could, given the right circumstances, be used successfully to take a *Tyrannosaurus rex*. The act of hunting *T. rex* requires a special kind of hunter using an extremely effective rifle with which the hunter is expertly proficient. Circumstances and exceptions aside, when pursuing *Tyrannosaurus rex*, the simplest advice is to choose the most powerful rifle that you can shoot quickly and accurately. Choose a rifle you trust and be sure to practice with it frequently.

Proper weapon choice is imperative when pursuing *Tyrannosaurus rex* because it is a creature unlike any a hunter is likely to have stalked before. It is nearly impossible to fully comprehend how large and powerful a big *T. rex* really is and how much skin, muscle and bone must be penetrated to reach the vitals of such a beast. Finding out that one's weapon is somehow lacking while facing a tyrannosaur is likely to be quite disconcerting... and terminal.

To make matters worse, to suggest that tyrannosaurs are quick to charge does not begin to describe the danger. Just as a spring robin (a descendant of Theropod dinosaurs like *T. rex*) strikes at an earthworm the moment it detects it, if a tyrannosaur can sense your presence, whether by sight, sound, smell or otherwise, it is already striking at you (note: a tyrannosaur's sense of smell is better than that of a tracking dog). The hunter can only hope that the dagger-toothed super-predator decides to toy with them a bit. If not, the tyrannosaur will offer no warning whatsoever. Sensing danger or even just a quick snack, a tyrannosaur will not hesitate to demonstrate why it is called *Rex*, a title it well deserves. *Tyrannosaurus rex* is a different kind of predator than those to which we are accustomed, as they are built on an altogether different scale. And, scale is important.

Consider this: A typical adult *Tyrannosaurus rex* weighs approximately 9 tons. That is about 20% larger than the *T. rex* featured in Stephen Spielberg's *Jurassic Park* movies. A large adult *T. rex* is equal in size to the largest bull elephant ever seen in Africa (Bush/Savannah elephant), 12 tons.

Certainly, there are those who would suggest that I am exaggerating the size of *T. rex*. I can only assure you that I am not. In point of fact, the average *T. rex* is a muscle bound behemoth and an indescribable terror. Even if they were smaller than I suggest, they would still be too large to fathom.

Having said that, the all-time record holder *T. rex* is a 16.9 ton (33,800 pound) beast standing 17.3' at the hip and 53' in length; its skull measures 80" in length and, despite its great size, it can sprint at 20 mph. Regardless of the size of the *T. rex* it is important to remember that these giant beasts will not be charging you just to scare you off; *Tyrannosaurus rex* will have harmful intent.

Tyrannosaurus rex are immense predators with highly efficient bird-like brains, more power at their disposal than an elephant, greater nutritional (read: protein) requirements than a large pride of lions and, when they are hungry, they have the weapons and ability to do something about it. Given all of this, one can begin to comprehend just what a challenge successfully taking a *T. rex* is and why it is so very dangerous, and alluring.

Please note: I will gladly be the first to tell all comers that I am not the foremost expert in the stalking or hunting of tyrannosaurs. However, I can say, with absolute surety, that I have as much experience stalking these predators as any living person. In addition to that, there are the countless hours I have spent studying full size, fully fleshed out *T. rex* mounts and models for effective shot angles and general anatomical study. I think, therefore, it is fair to suggest that my input regarding the selection of a rexGun is, at the very least, worthy of consideration.

I recall the first *Tyrannosaurus rex* that I ever saw; it was, interestingly enough, chasing butterflies, at least they looked like butterflies. It was the first opportunity that I ever had to lay eyes on a live *T. rex*; I was somewhat in awe. The grace and speed of its movement surprised me. It almost seemed impossible that such an immense creature could move so effortlessly, lunging and twisting to snap at the fluttering living toys with which it was playing.

But then, a young hadrosaur, vaguely the color of rust, came springing from the trees that surrounded the clearing in which the *T. rex* was playing, unaware of the danger ahead of it, seeming only to flee from some invisible terror that was behind it, somewhere in the trees. Its worries would not trouble the hadrosaur ever again.

The *T. rex*, an ever alert predatory giant, stepped quickly to its right and with lighting speed twisted its great hulking body toward its prey, every muscle in its thick powerful neck flexing and bulging as it brought its gapping maw of dagger-like teeth down upon the neck of the panicked beast. The teeth of the *T. rex* closed around the hadrosaur's neck, penetrating its thick skin and neck muscles almost effortlessly. Instantly the hadrosaur was dead, its neck broken, the great hulk of its body swinging forward with the momentum generated by its running. Yet, the *T. rex*, never losing its death grip on the neck of the beast, merely took half a step with its left foot to overcome the momentum and bring its prey to a final rest. It was an incredible event to witness, one that changed my view of *T. rex* forever.

I will never forget how the movement of tyrannosaur's every giant muscle was clearly visible beneath its magnificent skin. Its coloration, some combination of grey and brown, was so dark that light seemed to get lost within it and yet, its skin was almost shiny. I can best describe its skin as being like that of a clean wet African cape buffalo, but with more texture to it.

A *T. rex* is an almost mesmerizing sight; one could get lost in its beauty, forgetting that it is a great and mighty predator and that the very fact that you are witnessing this scene means that you are in almost certain danger.

An interesting point to consider is that *Tyrannosaurus rex* are probably the apex land predator of all time, much like African lion are the apex land predator in present-day Africa.

Consider that a single large male lion, weighing only 400 pounds, can take down a 1,600 pound Cape buffalo and that, when properly motivated, a record-size lion, weighing upwards of 500 pounds, can take down a rhinoceros weighing in excess of 3,000 pounds. Following the same pattern of logic, it is not unreasonable to suggest that a single large *T. rex* might take on prey weighing as much as 50 tons; a record size *T. rex* could likely take anything that has ever walked. This does not even take in to account the fact that tyrannosaurs are often social animals; facing a family or pack of *T. rex* is a terrifying proposition beyond words.

Of course, there are other land predators that could give *Tyrannosaurus rex* a good run for their title and are deserving of honorable mention. One such beast is the vicious *Spinosaurus aegyptiacus*; the record holder, at nearly 15 tons, thanks to the species lighter build, reached a length of approximately 70'. Similarly, there are other monstrous land predators that approach and even surpass the length of *Tyrannosaurus rex*. Among them are such terrors as *Tyrannotitan* and a trio of killing cousins- *Giganotosaurus*, *Mapusaurus* and *Carcharodontosaurus*. There are others, to be sure, but none that can match the combination of size and strength found in *T. rex*.

There is one important point that must be made before I continue. I have made a point, thus far, of referring to *Tyrannosaurus rex* and their competitors as land predators. This is very intentional as there is an important distinction between land and sea. Aquatic predators differ greatly from those we are discussing and are not likely to be considered, by many, as game for hunting.

However, there is one type of predator that has successfully blurred the line between predators of the land and those of the sea, and other waterways, so successfully that even *Tyrannosaurus rex* must be wary of them. I refer, of course, to crocodilians.

Crocodilians have, in their various forms, hunted nearly every type of environment in which the world has ever offered up prey. While nearly all crocodilians are of little concern to Tyrannosaurus rex, except perhaps as a snack, there is one crocodilian that humbles the mighty *T. rex*. It is *Sarcosuchus imperator*, the giant Crocodile, the greatest crocodilian of them all.

Sarcosuchus imperator can grow so large that even the largest and most powerful of land predators is fair game if they venture too close to the shores that *S. imperator* calls home. The *S. imperator* record holder is 68' in length, but as with *T. rex* it is not the length that gets you. That giant crocodile weighs a titanic 24.5 tons. Its overall mass is as much greater than the record *T. rex* as the record *T. rex* is greater than the record elephant. Even the second place *S. imperator* record holder is a thing to behold; at 65' long, it weighs 22.9 tons.

While I have no doubt that, in some circumstances, a large *Tyrannosaurus rex* could make quick work of an attacking *Sarcosuchus imperator*, I am equally certain that in other circumstances the reverse it true. So you see, even *Tyrannosaurus rex* are not entirely free of fear from predation.

I mention the above to make a very important point: *Tyrannosaurus rex,* though fearsome, are not fearless giants wandering the world with total impunity, caring of nothing except from where the next meal will come. While they may have less to fear than most, they too are aware of the dangers and perils around them; it is that very awareness and the resulting alertness necessitated by it that makes hunting *T. rex* so extremely dangerous.

Perhaps, because the human hunter sets out after *Tyrannosaurus rex* with forethought and intent, with total awareness of the risks and dangers involved, hunting not out of necessity but for sport, it is the human hunter that deserves the title *Predator rex*.

Part 2: Terminal Medicine

27

Given the nearly incomprehensible size of *Tyrannosaurus rex*, determining what cartridges and bullets might be used to effectively take one can be tricky. To aid the would-be *T. rex* hunter in this decision, I have developed a formula that can be used to estimate the effectiveness of a cartridge/bullet combination and rank, for comparison purposes, its ability to take a *T. rex*. I call this formula Terminal Medicine (T.Rx).

To vividly illustrate the usefulness of the T.Rx formula, Table 1 lists cartridges drawn from many arenas by T.Rx value. They range from antiquated cartridges of the era of the African

Great White Hunter to modern hunting rounds and even military rounds originally intended for non-sporting purposes. I have included some custom cartridges and hand-loads. However, the rexGun list is not without its omissions, both intentional and unintentional, and many cartridges appear on the list more than once using different bullets to demonstrate how bullet selection affects overall performance. The rexGun list does give an excellent sample of the available cartridges that may be pressed into service against *Tyrannosaurus rex*.

303 Brit., 9.3x74R, 470 NE

The appropriate amount of Terminal Medicine varies from species to species. To establish a point of reference, Table 2 offers a comparison of proper T.Rx values for *T. rex* (predator) and African elephant (prey) based on live weight.

Truly gigantic creatures, such as elephants and tyrannosaurs, defy all previous predictive performance models. To remedy this situation I have developed my T.Rx formula specifically for such creatures. It does seem to work for the smaller beasts as well, but it was developed for the giants.

In truth, tyrannosaurs are not completely dissimilar to African bull elephants in terms of bullet resistance. While I do differentiate between them as predator and game animal respectively, such differentiation is negated when discussing wounded or agitated bull elephants and the violent, often predatory, behavior occasionally exhibited by them. Pound for pound, I would say in that context the two are essentially equal in terms of Terminal Medicine requirements. However, one must remember that *T. rex* are, on average, about 50% larger than African Bush/Savannah elephant bulls. True, the *Tyrannosaurus rex* lacks the thick, bullet slowing, "honeycomb" that protects the brain of the elephant, but they are much larger than elephants with far more extremely dense predator muscle surrounding a much smaller brain. The jaw is slightly "honeycombed" to allow for greater fracture resistance when biting, but the skull is rigid and dense and will transfer any shockwaves that can reach the skull near the brain much more efficiently than will the skull of an elephant. *Tyrannosaurus rex* also have a thick bony plate protecting the heart from some shot angles.

Think of a *T. rex* as a cross between an African lion, an African Cape buffalo, a Nile crocodile, the largest imaginable elephant and a Stirton's Thunder Bird (Dromornis stirtoni).

As if that image alone were not terrifying enough, make the creature in your mind 50% larger.

To make matters worse, tyrannosaurs are descended from archosaurs; as such, they have the extreme resistance to death that all creatures descended from archosaurs (including birds and crocodiles) seem to have. Think of it as a somewhat larger than normal "grey area" that exists between alive and dead.

Table 4, Weight to T.Rx, contains two distinct ranges of T.Rx values for each weight category. The lower value is for game animals, such as elephant. The higher T.Rx value is intended for more dangerous situations, such as hunting predators or following up agitated or dangerous game animals. It is very important to recognize the distinction between passive game animals and those which have turned aggressive.

It is important, when selecting a rexGun cartridge and rifle, to consider that in spite of their great size one is not likely to take a shot at a *Tyrannosaurus rex* much beyond 120 yards. Most shots are likely to be taken at much closer ranges than that, 10 to 40 yards is more likely. Therefore, long-range performance is not a major consideration in the selection process.

Hunting *T. rex* in open country is simply not wise. Grass has not yet evolved in their world. Without the vast grass fields we are accustomed to in modern Africa to conceal an approach, your options are quite limited. You really don't want to make it easy for the tyrannosaur(s) to pick out your location after the initial shot. And you certainly don't want them to know that you are coming before you take that shot. *T. rex* have such excellent senses that the hunter really needs the sights, sounds and smells of the rain forest, jungle or thick-scrub to mask their presence as they approach; that equates to close quarters encounters.

Regardless, to shoot dangerous game from extreme distances is rather unsporting; even *T. rex*, are not truly dangerous unless they are quite close.

Selecting a rexGun cartridge can be quite simple if you already know what cartridge you prefer for elephant, as they are of similar scale. By that I mean that the terminal ballistics required, such as depth of penetration, for each are similar.

Before I complete that thought I must explain that, personally, I prefer to prepare for worst case scenarios. In the case of *T. rex* that means penetration; their very tough skin is one and a half to two inches thick in most places. Their hearts are protected from the forward shot angles by very dense bone plates (not hollow ones) ranging from two to three inches thick.

A good rexGun bullet must be able to penetrate those obstacles and still drive straight and true for another three to four feet through extremely

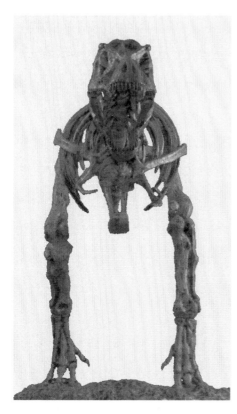

dense tissue and muscle, as that is the length of a *T. rex* heart on the long axis.

If a rifle and cartridge can achieve those results under those circumstances and leave a decent wound channel as well, then in my opinion, it is an excellent choice for a rexGun.

To determine if your preferred choices of rifle, cartridge and bullet used for elephant are adequate for *Tyrannosaurus rex*, simply find the T.Rx value of your preferred elephant rifle cartridge on the rexGun Cartridge Table (Table 1). Find the T.Rx value of your preferred cartridge on the *Tyrannosaurus rex* T.Rx Table (Table 2) to determine how effective your cartridge is likely to be (Minimum, Adequate, Proper, Improved, Superior, Stopping) when used against *T. rex*.

If you find that your preferred elephant rifle cartridge is already enough for *T. rex*, and you are certain that your choice of bullet has adequate penetration characteristics, and you are confident in your abilities with the rifle, then you are set.

Things are only slightly more complicated if you desire the same level of performance on *T. rex* as you get on elephant with your preferred elephant rifle combination.

In this case, find the T.Rx value of your preferred elephant rifle cartridge on the rexGun Cartridge Table (Table 1). Then add 16 points (+/- 1 point) to that value.

Look for cartridges on the rexGun Cartridge Table (Table 1) that match this new adjusted T.Rx value and, provided you are careful to look for a cartridge with similar ballistic characteristics (bullet speed, etc.) to your preferred elephant rifle cartridge, then this new cartridge will deliver the performance you desire when hunting a *Tyrannosaurus rex*. Table 3, Terminal Effectiveness Comparison, provides several specific examples.

To clarify, the iconic 470 Nitro Express cartridge (T.Rx 85) performs against *Tyrannosaurus rex* similarly to how the 450/400 Nitro Express 3¼" (T.Rx 68) performs on elephant; while the legendary 416 Rigby (T.Rx 79) performs on *T. rex* similarly to how the 375 Holland & Holland Magnum (T.Rx 63) performs on elephant.

These are excellent cartridges with long proven histories behind them. But, are they enough gun for *T. rex*?

The answer is: certainly, they are. Though, I would suggest that they are probably the lower limit for safe use in a rexGun.

My suggestion that the cartridges just mentioned may represent the lower limit for use on T. rex does not in any way disqualify those cartridges from consideration for use in a rexGun. As I have said, they are enough gun.

To explain further, in the heyday of dangerous game hunting – the first half of the twentieth century, proper gentleman hunters often outfitted themselves for safari with rifles chambered for cartridges from the 450-470 group or one of the big 400's (416 Rigby, 425 Westley Richards, etc.). While, in contrast, the professional hunters often chose something a bit lighter, such as one of the light 400's (450/400, 404 Jeffrey, etc.) or a 375 H&H. These two groups approached the hunting of dangerous game from different perspectives.

Generally speaking, the safari hunter wanted a weapon that offered as much Terminal Medicine (though they did not call it that) as they could get in a rifle that they could handle reasonably well. The thinking was that this choice would best ensure their safe return home at the end of the safari.

The professional hunter more often wanted the lightest weapon that could be relied upon to do the job well. This reduced fatigue and gave the professional much greater control of the weapon, which tends to enhance speed and accuracy. This allowed for more shots, more often and that meant more game in the bag which equates to greater income.

Both viewpoints are just as valid; many large dangerous beasts have fallen to each of those groups of cartridges.

Speaking of which, there has long been a question within each of those groups over the best weapon design. Some choose single barrel bolt-action repeating rifles while others prefer double rifles.

The bolt-action rifles have such excellent inherent accuracy that the users of such rifles can often justify choosing cartridges based almost solely upon the penetration characteristics of the bullet that they fire. Thereby assuring that, if a good shot is made, the bullet will penetrate through any obstacles encountered to reach deep enough to strike the exact target point desired. Further, the bolt-action rifle design does offer an advantage over the double rifle in terms of ammunition capacity which can be quite important during some emergency situations.

Others choose double rifles which have a bit less inherent accuracy but generally fire larger, heavier bullets that destroy any obstacles they encounter, rather than just passing through them. The double rifles heavy bullet is less likely to strike the exact point desired but is accurate enough to strike the vitals of nearly any dangerous beast. And it will do more damage along the way and to those vitals when it does connect. The double rifle design does offer an advantage over the bolt-action in that it offers a much shorter window of time between the first and second shots. Against dangerous game, that quick second shot can be the difference between life and death for the hunter and the game if the first shot fails to drop the beast. Though rare, if the first shot results in a misfire, then the second may be the first to strike the animal and therefore needs to come as quickly as possible. Against no other creature are these issues of such importance as when facing the fearsome *Tyrannosaurus rex.*

Each point of view is equally valid. The individual hunter must choose, for themselves, what type of rifle and power level best fits their individual shooting and hunting style.

If you feel that a 450/400 Nitro Express 3¼" is enough gun for hunting elephant and that your 470 Nitro Express is perfectly adequate for following up an agitated 10 ton bull elephant in any and all conditions, then certainly your 470 is equally adequate to serve as your primary weapon for hunting a similarly sized *Tyrannosaurus rex.*

Ferlach 470 Nitro Express Double Rifle

If you do consider your 470 Nitro Express to be enough gun for anything, then you will be happy to know that you are not alone. Joseph Lang, inventor of the 470 Nitro Express, and Rigby's designers agreed, as did the legendary John Taylor, who said, in his book <u>African Rifles & Cartridges</u>, of the 450-470 Nitro Express group of cartridges: "You may tackle the heaviest and most dangerous beast in existence in the worst cover imaginable, with any one of these calibres without suffering a single qualm of nervousness-they will not let you down."

Of course, John Taylor did not have *Tyrannosaurus rex* in mind when he made that statement. I suspect that a great many *T. rex* hunters would feel more comfortable with a rexGun that offers a bit more power than those just mentioned - especially when an adult *T. rex* is less than one hundred feet away.

For the gentleman safari hunter a 500 Nitro Express 3" (T.Rx 97) double rifle is quite sporting, offering a level of performance on *Tyrannosaurus rex* that is quite similar to that of the 450 Nitro Express (T.Rx 81) on elephant.

For those gentlemen who prefer a bolt-action rifle, the 465 Holland & Holland Magnum (T.Rx 93) is an excellent choice, performing against *T. rex* quite like the 400 H&H Magnum (T.Rx 77) performs against elephant; very sporting indeed!

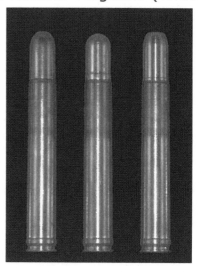

458 Lott cartridges Woodleigh, A-Square, and Barnes solids

A recent development of significance to those of us of more modest means, Jack Lott's Wildcat cartridge, the 458 Lott (T.Rx 92), is now commercially available in affordable bolt-action rifles along with factory ammunition featuring quality jacketed solids, monolithic solids and even Sledgehammers. With performance on *T. rex* that is similar to that of the 416 Taylor (T.Rx 76) on elephant, the 458 Lott is perhaps the first true "factory" rexGun. A rifle so chambered would be an excellent choice as a lightweight yet effective rifle for the properly outfitted adventurer exploring dinosaur territory.

I am fully aware that the 460 Wheatherby (T.Rx 108) cartridge does pre-date the 458 Lott as a production cartridge, but, in my opinion, the 460 has far too much recoil for all but a very few hunters to use it repeatedly while maintaining accuracy, reliability and quickness.

A great many cartridges offer performance against *Tyrannosaurus rex* that is similar to the performance of the big 400's and the 450-470 Nitro group against elephant. It is important to remember that no single 450-470 Nitro Elephant Gun cartridge really outshined the others, not even my beloved 470 Nitro Express. The same is true of the big 400's. They were all truly excellent against elephant, as are the equivalent cartridges against *Tyrannosaurus rex.*

Similarly, the selection of a proper rexGun cartridge is more dependent upon which is available in a rifle design you shoot well and trust with your life than it is upon which cartridge is better. Each of the suitable cartridges is magnificent in its own way.

Even so, a great many hunters would not consider going after *Tyrannosaurus rex*, even a small one, with anything less than a 577 Nitro Express (T.Rx 121). Certainly, there is nothing wrong with such a choice, provided the hunter is very skilled with such a heavy and powerful weapon and can manage its recoil. Against *Tyrannosaurus rex*, speed, bullet placement and the bullet's ability to reach and damage the vitals are what count. If the hunter can handle such a powerful weapon quickly and place the bullet properly, then the 577 N.E.'s bullet will certainly reach the vitals of a *T. rex*. The 577 N.E.'s performance on game is legendary, but remember what John Taylor said, in <u>African Rifles & Cartridges</u>, "…the enormous power of the .577 is really unnecessary." When speaking about the 577 Taylor said: "Long years of experience have shown that the various weapons in the .450-.500 group have all the power necessary to enable you to safely tackle any animal anywhere." Think of a .577 as a second rifle. In a bolt-action rifle, similar results, to that of the 577 N.E., can be had from the mighty 500 A-square (T.Rx 122).

Regardless of what cartridge one selects for their own rexGun, what truly matters is that the bullets are where they need to be, when they need to be there. If they are not, then even a 700 Nitro Express (T.Rx 160) or 600 Overkill (T.Rx 180) will fail miserably against *Tyrannosaurus rex*.

As with all things, there must be balance. In this case it is the balance between practical terminal effectiveness, which is where the Terminal Medicine formula and the Weight to T.Rx Table become so useful, and the hunter's ability to use the weapon effectively.

I cannot hope to determine what the perfect rexGun is for all hunters in all situations. Each hunter will have different expectations of their rexGun, be they ammunition capacity or mode of operation. Hunters must consider their own desires, abilities and limitations when choosing a rexGun.

Author & 470 Capstick

My own desires and limitations have resulted in my large and/or dangerous game rifles being a 416 Rigby (T.Rx 79) bolt-action, a 470 Nitro Express (T.Rx 85) double, and a 470 Capstick (T.Rx 98) bolt action, each of which can serve as a perfectly adequate rexGun.

You must consider your own desires, skills and limitations carefully when choosing your rexGun, remembering that biggest is not always best - not for lion, not for elephant and not for *Tyrannosaurus rex*.

I believe that if there were to be a sudden dramatic increase in *T. rex* populations, thereby causing rexGun ownership to become commonplace among hunters and others, the CZ 550 Magnum rifle (a slightly improved version of the legendary BRNO 602), chambered for the 458 Lott cartridge (T.Rx 92), would quickly become the most popular and commonly encountered rexGun, world wide.

Semi-custom CZ 550 Magnum, 416 Rigby

While some, like me, might prefer to see those CZ 550 Magnum rifles chambered for the powerful, yet magnificently well balanced and "sniper accurate", 470 Capstick (T.Rx 98) cartridge and a great many would be better served by the mild recoil and superb penetration of the 416 Rigby (T.Rx 79), few could argue with such a choice.

The long history of reliability and durability attributed to the CZ 550 Magnum (BRNO 602) rifle coupled with the ability that rifles chambered for the 458 Lott cartridge have to safely shoot the globally available supplies of 458 Winchester Magnum (T.Rx 79) ammunition all but assures my belief.

Let us, for a moment, also consider those extremely powerful rifle cartridges that are truly more suitable for backup use against *T. rex* than they are in actual hunting weapons. As rexGuns go, these are emergency use weapons only. They are, each in their own way, much too powerful and/or unwieldy for general use. There are many schools of thought on this subject and in the following I will address but a few.

- The Speed Freaks could not hope for more than the 475 A&M Magnum (T.Rx 134) and its 500-grain bullet travelling at nearly 3,000 fps.

- The Number Crunchers believe that the 577 Tyrannosaur (T.Rx 148), with its 750-grain bullet travelling at the magic speed, 2,400 fps, is ballistically perfect.

- Still others, whom we will call Old School, are certain that stopping rifles peaked in 1902 with the completion of the first 600 Nitro Express (T.Rx 139) double rifle, sending down-range a 900-grain bullet at a modest 1,950 fps.

- Then we come to the Antiquarians, people who think smokeless powder was a big mistake and that no better stopping rifle than the 4-bore (T.Rx 140), and its 2000-grain lead thumper travelling 1,300 fps, has ever been developed.

- For the CiMFC (Camouflage is My Favorite Color) crowd, nothing less than a 50 BMG (T.Rx 138) repeater with an 18" barrel sending a 600-grain slug at no less than 2,700 fps is acceptable.

Which of these groups has it right? Well, they all do! Each of their logic-trains is right on track; it is just that their trains are all riding along on different tracks. Each of those cartridges just mentioned is so staggeringly powerful that a properly timed, well-placed shot by any one of them cannot help but drop any beast that has ever walked. That is, unless it is simply not that animal's day to die. To further clarify, John Taylor described, in <u>African Rifles & Cartridges</u>, "A 600 will split a Cape buffalo's head open like smashing a watermelon on a rock." And, "600's are more powerful than any rifle ever needs to be".

When compared to the cartridges just mentioned, many of the cartridges on the rexGun list may seem, at first glance, to be a bit light for use against *Tyrannosaurus rex*. I assure you that this is not true; given proper bullet design and load selection, many cartridges much lighter than those would do quite nicely in a rexGun and many more would do quite well against smaller tyrannosaurs, or perhaps even an adult Albertosaur, Carnotaur, Gorgosaur or Utahraptor. Generally, such creatures only reach 20 to 30 feet in length and weigh less than 5 tons as mature adults.

Truly, those smaller super-predators are a good place for a would-be *T. rex* hunter to "cut their teeth" and gain some useful experience against a much less massive, yet fully developed, adult beast before jumping into their first *T. rex* hunt.

Italian 9.3x74R Double Rifle

Many hunters have forgotten just how easy it is to kill even enormous animals with proper bullet placement and adequate penetration. Comparatively modest cartridges such as 9.3x74R and 375

Holland & Holland Magnum will reach an elephant's vitals from most angles and they will fully penetrate an elephant's skull. But, should the shots be hurried and the bullets placed poorly, history has shown us that even an average elephant will run far, far away with a pair of 600 Nitro bullets in its gut.

The point is this: if you cannot put the bullets where they need to be, then do not go after *Tyrannosaurus rex*.

In getting the bullets where they need to be, the importance of penetration cannot be overstated.

Without question the 416 Rigby and its brethren (T.Rx 78-79) can penetrate deeply enough to reach the vitals of any creature that has ever walked. Such cartridges have demonstrated time and again the perfect balance of terminal performance and penetration that is achieved by a 400-grain bullet of just over 400-caliber moving along at 2,400-fps.

That formula, much like the 470's 500-grain bullet at 2,150 fps formula, is not questioned; it is not debated; it is the stuff of legend.

When discussing those legendary cartridges we are, after all, talking about rifle cartridges that fire bullets capable of easily penetrating quarter-inch steel plate.

When a rexGun, 470 N.E., and ¼" steel plate meet!

And, let us not forget that it was a 416 Rigby that felled the largest land animal taken with a firearm in the 20th century, a 12-ton Angolan elephant that stood nearly 13-ft tall at the shoulder. That elephant was larger than an average *Tyrannosaurus rex*.

While caliber, in terms of cross-sectional area and bullet weight, and bullet speed are important considerations; against elephant and *Tyrannosaurus rex,* penetration is always king.

The larger the caliber and the greater the weight of the bullet the better the results will be when the bullet and game meet. But, if that bullet cannot reach the beasts vitals because it is too short and fat for its weight to do so, you might as well be throwing rocks.

The very worst time for a hunter to learn that the cartridge or bullet they chose lacks adequate penetration is when battling large dangerous game; they don't get any larger or more dangerous than *T. rex*.

History and experience have shown that the best cartridges for dangerous game are those that offer the largest caliber and bullet weight while retaining enough penetration for the game in question.

There are bullet/cartridge combinations that have adequate penetration for hunting *T. rex,* such as the traditional 9.3's (T.Rx 53-56) and 375's (T.Rx 60-63), but lack the terminal performance, due to insufficient caliber and bullet weight, to reliably bring down such a massive predator.

Bigger bullets make bigger holes and bigger holes cause more rapid blood loss. The more rapidly a beast loses blood the less time it has to kill you. It is that simple.

Nonetheless, the larger the diameter of the bullet, the more it must weigh and/or the faster it must travel in order to retain sufficient penetration characteristics.

With enough weight behind a bullet of large enough diameter comes the ability to break or shatter large bones instead of poking neat little holes through them.

A 450 Nitro Express fires a 480-grain 458-calliber bullet and will break an elephant's shoulder bones every time.

A 375 H&H fires a 300-grain 375-calliber bullet that pokes nice clean holes through elephant shoulder bones (only rarely breaking them) but with much deeper penetration than the 450.

The 450's bullet is capable of penetrating as deeply as the 375's bullet, but to do so, it must be pushed much faster than it is from a 450 N.E.

Long and skinny bullets always out-penetrate short and fat bullets when weight and speed are equal. A short-fat bullet can be pushed fast enough to penetrate as deeply as a long-skinny bullet of the same weight, but it requires that the short-fat bullet be travelling much faster – though in some cases, so much faster that it is simply not practical in the field.

It does take less gunpowder to push a larger diameter bullet of the same weight to an equal speed as a narrower bullet because the larger diameter bullet has a greater cross-sectional area and therefore offers a greater surface area at the rear of the bullet upon which the cartridge's expanding gases can act against, pushing the bullet more easily.

This principle can be more easily explained by a simple analogy: It is easier to push with a hand than it is with a finger. But, a finger penetrates more easily than a hand.

There are so many factors involved in terminal ballistics that finding a proper balance of all of these cartridge/bullet characteristics is, in some ways, a matter of personal preference.

As previously mentioned, my rexGuns are a 470 Nitro Express double (T.Rx 85) and a 470 Capstick bolt-action (T.Rx 98). By my thinking those cartridges offer the perfect balance of usability and performance on *Tyrannosaurus rex*.

The 470 Capstick offers the largest caliber & bullet weight for terminal performance in a cartridge that offers the largest ammunition capacity available in a manageable rifle while guaranteeing enough bullet speed to ensure adequate penetration for even the tough shots on *T. rex*, approximately six feet of penetration.

Custom Winchester Model 70, 470 Capstick

Admittedly, there were times that I questioned my 470 Nitro doubles' ability to perform against *T. rex*. That is, until I witnessed the performance of modern flat-nose homogenous-sold bullets on game and discovered that they can be safely fired in my rifle – now I have no doubts.

Ferlach 470 Nitro Express Double Rifle

My double favors Barnes banded solids and, having witnessed that bullet's terminal performance and the performance improvement that it offers over that of the classic jacketed tapered-nose solids (exactly as my T.Rx formula predicts), I no longer have any qualms about taking my 470 against anything, even the mightiest *Tyrannosaurus rex*.

However, every rifle is different. It is important to have your rifle inspected by a qualified gunsmith before trying to switch to homogenous-solids in your double rifle. These bullets have no "give" and can seriously damage an undersized barrel.

Once again, I must point out that my Terminal Medicine formula is designed for non-expanding and non-deforming bullets. What I mean by that is that the bullets must not expand or deform upon impact with or during penetration in very large dense beasts. Modern homogenous-solids and the classic steel-jacketed solids are fine examples.

The formula is simply not designed for use with expanding bullets. But, it does work adequately with lead, hardened lead and lightly jacketed bullets. These bullets regularly deform a bit but they often offer good penetration characteristics.

A simple modification of the resulting value is needed to compensate for the loss of Terminal Medicine as a result of the deformation of the bullet upon impact and/or during penetration.

Reduce lead bullet T.Rx values by 40% and lightly hardened lead bullets by 30%. Hard lead bullets (very hard, but not brittle) are reduced by 20%. Common jacketed lead bullets are reduced by 10%.

These modifications to the Terminal Medicine value make it possible to compare classic cartridges, firing their original bullets, to their modern counterparts, firing modern bullets. For example, the old black-powder bore-rifles can be compared to modern big-bore rifles and rexGuns with reasonable accuracy.

When discussing terminal ballistics, no system of measured comparison can be absolute or perfect. The Terminal Medicine (T.Rx) formula comes reasonably close.

In addition to *Tyrannosaurus rex*, the Terminal Medicine formula can be used to select a rifle/ cartridge for hunting other game as well. From white-tailed deer and leopard all the way up to gigantic super-predators, such as the previously mentioned *Spinosaurus aegyptiacus* and *Sarcosuchus imperator*.

Simply match the T.Rx value of the cartridge/bullet combination to the weight and behavior of the animal being pursued on the Weight to T.Rx Table (Table 4). This will provide the hunter with the best chance of success while limiting the risk of being eaten by a very angry, wounded super-predator.

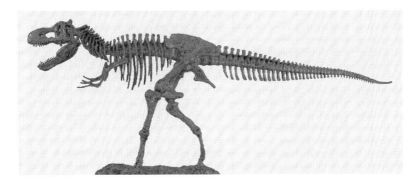

This sequence of photographs show the
effect of a 400-grain, 416-caliber
Hornady Solid bullet fired from a 416
Rigby rifle in to ¼" Steel Plate

Notice the effect of the bullet on the ¼"
Steel Plate – it literally throws the plate
in to the air.

The holes made in the ¼" Steel Plate
by the Hornady solids are larger than
caliber and are clearly visible.

Part 3: Laws & Formulae

This section contains materials used for reference. I have provided the relevant Laws of Ballistic Dynamics, as I understand them, as well as all of the necessary formulas used to determine the Terminal Medicine (T.Rx) value.

Table 1, *rexGun Cartridges*, lists many cartridges and the pertinent data for each, sorted by T.Rx value.

Table 2, *Species Specific T.Rx Values*, shows the T.Rx values suggested for *Tyrannosaurus rex* and African elephant sorted by weight class.

Table 3, *Terminal Effectiveness Comparison*, is a predicted equivalent performance comparison of appropriate cartridges for *T. rex* and African elephant. It expresses the level of performance one might expect against T. rex with a given cartridge by supplying an example of a cartridge that offers similar performance on African elephant.

Table 4, *Weight to T.Rx*, suggests an appropriate T.Rx value for game animals, prey and predators, based on their weight.

I have also included some interesting and useful pictures as well as a simple Target Areas diagram of a tyrannosaur.

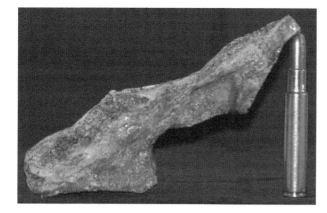

Cast of a full-size T. rex brain cavity shown with a 416 Rigby cartridge. A small target indeed!

Laws of Ballistic Dynamics:

1.   As Bullet Weight increases, Penetration Depth increases; the inverse is also true.

2.   As Bullet Speed increases, Penetration Depth increases; the inverse is also true.

3.   As Bullet Diameter increases (by Caliber, or resulting from impact), Penetration Depth decreases; the inverse is also true.

4.   As Bullet Diameter increases (by Caliber, or resulting from impact), the rate of Kinetic Energy release increases; the inverse is also true.

5.   As the rate of Kinetic Energy release increases, Wound Diameter increases; the inverse is also true.

6.   As BIZ* increases, Wound Diameter increases; the inverse is also true.

Note: The effects of the Laws of Ballistic Dynamics are cumulative; they may compound and/or counteract one another.

*Bullet Impact Zone measurement: (BIZ)

BIZ is a measure of how effectively a specific solid bullet design will impact a target animal. It is determined by the shape of the bullet at the forward-most section or tip.

Generally, a lower BIZ value indicates greater penetration, while a higher value indicates greater wound diameter and Kinetic Energy release upon impact.

BIZ is calculated by averaging the minimum Bullet Impact Zone diameter (at the forward-most tip of the bullet) and the diameter of the bullet exactly one-quarter inch (¼") back from the tip and then dividing the resulting value by the distance between them (0.25). The result is then modified by the overall diameter of the bullet, where a 0.458 semi-sphere or round ball has a BIZ value of 1.0.

The minimum bullet diameter is the smallest measurable diameter at the tip of the bullet. It can prove difficult to calculate for some jacketed solids, and it can be zero. If the bullet tip is perfectly round/spherical the value is certainly zero, whereas if the bullet has a broad meplat, or flattened tip, the value will be quite large.

Unadjusted BIZ value =

$$\frac{\text{Average BIZ Diameter}}{\text{BIZ Length}} \quad \begin{array}{l}\text{(100ths of an inch)}\\\text{(100ths of an inch)}\end{array}$$

For example, consider a .458 A-square monolithic solid bullet. The A-square bullet has a semi-spherical nose; the Minimum Bullet Impact diameter is 0. The diameter of the bullet ¼ inch (.25 inches) from the tip is .444 inches. Obtain the average value by adding the two values (0.0 + 0.444 = 0.444) and dividing by two (0.444 ÷ 2 = 0.222).

To obtain the Unadjusted BIZ value for this bullet, divide the Average BIZ Diameter (0.222 inches) by BIZ Length (0.25 inches) (0.222 ÷ 0.25 = 0.888). The unadjusted BIZ measurement of this bullet is 0.888.

Following are these calculations notated in standard mathematics:

Average BIZ Diameter =

$$\frac{0.0" + 0.444"}{2} = 0.222"$$

Unadjusted BIZ value =

$$\frac{0.222"}{0.25"} = 0.888"$$

As the .458 A-square monolithic solid bullet is the base measure in the BIZ formula, its value (0.888") is treated as 1.000. Therefore, the Unadjusted BIZ value, 0.888", results in the base measure Adjusted BIZ value of 1.000 BIZ.

To determine the Adjusted BIZ value of any bullet other than the base measure .458 A-square monolithic solid, first calculate the Unadjusted BIZ value of the bullet. Then, using the base measure bullet values (0.888 / 1.000) adjust the new value algebraically, by cross-multiplication, to determine the Adjusted BIZ value of the new bullet.

For example, consider a .458 Woodleigh Solid. That bullet has an Unadjusted BIZ value of 0.875. Use cross-multiplication to determine the Adjusted BIZ value, where the Adjusted BIZ value = X:

Unadjusted BIZ: 0.888   x   0.875 .
Adjusted BIZ: 1.000 X

$0.875 \times 1.000 \div 0.888 = X$

The resulting value for X is 0.985. Therefore the Adjusted BIZ value for a .458 Woodleigh Solid bullet is 0.985.

In simplified form that calculation is - divide the new bullet Unadjusted BIZ value (0.875) by the default measure bullet Unadjusted BIZ value (0.888). The result will be the same Adjusted BIZ value (0.985) ($0.875 \div 0.888 = 0.985$).

Some additional examples:

A .416 A-square monolithic solid has an Unadjusted BIZ value of 0.807 and an Adjusted BIZ value of 0.908. (0.807 ÷ 0.888 = 0.908)

A .416 Woodleigh Solid has an Unadjusted BIZ value of 0.795 and an Adjusted BIZ value of 0.895. (0.795 ÷ 0.888 = 0.895)

Determining the Adjusted BIZ value of a solid bullet design may seem complicated, but that value is an absolutely critical part of the Terminal Medicine formula.

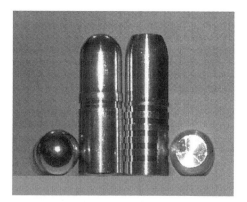

.475 bullets from A-square and Barnes showing the variance in the bullet impact zone on similarly constructed monolithic solids

Terminal Medicine formula: (T.Rx)

Comparing the effectiveness of different rifle cartridges can be quite tricky. Many such formulas exist, but none seems quite adequate when comparing the effectiveness of cartridges for use against truly massive game animals, such as African elephant and *Tyrannosaurus rex*. For these truly massive creatures I have developed the Terminal Medicine formula (abbreviated: T.Rx).

The T.Rx formula results in an easily managed numeric value for any given cartridge/bullet combination which can be used for comparison purposes and, subsequently, it may also be used to estimate effectiveness.

One of the key features of the T.Rx formula is that it amplifies the terminal ballistic effect of changes in load or bullet design, no matter how small, allowing for a more effective comparison of the loads available in any given cartridge.

The comparisons made possible by the T.Rx formula and the implications thereof do seem to be supported by historical evidence, thereby adding some measure of support to their validity.

For example: Historically, it is well known that the eminently respectable East Africa Professional Hunters' Association established 40-caliber as the minimum for hunting elephant.

Generally that would represent the 450/400 Nitro Express 3", which was, and still is, a highly respected cartridge.

The T.Rx value for the 450/400 3" cartridge, when loaded with a Woodleigh Solid, is 67, thereby establishing that T.Rx value as adequate for hunting any elephant (note: they did not differentiate between large and small elephants).

Similarly, the legendary 404 Jeffery, which is perhaps the most widely used of all the dangerous game rifle cartridges, also scores a 67 on the T.Rx scale as it was originally loaded.

These two cartridges were developed at around the same time in history for use in the same environments and for the same purposes. Neither outshined the other and they each earned much admiration and respect from those hunters who used them. In the hands of those who used both, these cartridges performed equally well.

Hence, historical precedent would seem to agree with the T.Rx formula, that a cartridge/bullet combination with a T.Rx value of 67 can be considered reasonable for use against even the largest African Elephant (which, as previously mentioned, weighed about 12 tons).

Another pair of grand old cartridges with long histories as fairly reliable light elephant rounds are the 375 Holland & Holland Magnums, Flanged and Belted, (T.Rx 60 or 63, depending upon the load).

The 375s have been used, if a bit less reliably, to take many large tuskers, though many consider them to be a bit under powered for that task and recommend them for use only on smaller elephants.

It does, therefore, seem reasonable to accept 60 and 63 as the minimum T.Rx for successful use on average and large African Elephant.

If we accept these values, along with those previously mentioned, this does seem to give a very natural T.Rx progression relative to elephant weights that is supported by historical precedent.

Further evidence that supports this assertion can be seen in the fact that, historically, cartridges that fall below the recommended minimum T.Rx value have been considered, by many, to be potentially unsafe and, quite possibly, inhumane for use against African elephant.

For example the T.Rx value of the exquisite 9.3x74R cartridge is 53-56 (depending upon the load). This cartridge has recorded a great many successes when used on elephant, but it has a long history of failures as well, just as its lower T.Rx values would seem to predict.

This cartridge and the 9.3x62 Mauser, which was a successful attempt to get terminal ballistics similar to the 9.3x74R in a bolt-action rifle, while quite capable of taking elephant, are generally considered to be more reliable when used on smaller jungle/forest elephants or sub-adult bush/savannah elephants.

Perhaps two better examples would be Bell's 318 Westley Richards (T.Rx 50) and Selous' 450 Express (T.Rx 50).

Those cartridges are certainly capable of taking elephant, as Bell and Selous have shown. Though neither has sufficient terminal ballistic performance to be considered ideal for hunting elephant; to that, both Bell and Selous agreed.

Historical precedent also supports that a cartridge with a T.Rx value somewhat higher than minimum is, generally, a more reliable performer and will serve better in heavy bush, against the charge of a wounded or otherwise agitated game animal or against extremely dangerous game – such as predators.

For such situations, I generally recommend choosing a cartridge that starts thirteen (+/- 1) points higher than the recommended minimum Game Animal T.Rx value.

It is possible for a cartridge to perform adequately beyond what is indicated by its T.Rx rating, but this requires very careful load and bullet selection as well as extremely accurate shooting.

This exception generally applies to heavy-for-caliber bullets that are travelling at optimum performance speeds of between 2,000 and 2,400 fps at impact.

Below that speed range, bullets require a higher BIZ value and/or greater weight to be genuinely effective. Of course, higher BIZ values and weight help at speeds above 2,000 fps too.

Bullet speeds higher than 2,400 fps, at impact, can suffer bullet and flight stability loss, causing tumbling, bullet failure or other erratic behavior.

Just as it is possible for a bullet to take game for which its T.Rx rating seems too low, it is also possible for a cartridge to perform adequately on game requiring much less T.Rx than the cartridge offers, though some consider this to be overkill.

I generally do not accept the overkill theory – that a cartridge with a T.Rx value beyond the Stopping level for the game being pursued may result in an overkill situation and that, if this occurs, terminal performance may suffer as a result. I am certain that no such reduction in terminal performance will occur in those situations. The 416 Rigby may not be the ideal cartridge for hunting white-tail deer, but it will certainly get the job done.

However, that does not deny the existence of overkill in weapon selection.

No hunter has ever needed, or will ever need (not even for the largest *Tyrannosaurus rex* in the thickest bush), more Terminal Medicine than the 577 Nitro Express (T.Rx 121) delivers. Most hunters would be much better served by far less Terminal Medicine than that.

I suspect that in most cases the real problem with overkill comes when a hunter is using too much gun for a specific hunting situation, which results when a hunter chooses a weapon that is just too much for them to handle. It is the hunter's own performance that suffers as a result.

You must know and respect your limitations, because with rexGuns, you get what you give, quite literally.

Remember, you cannot send a 900-grain bullet downrange at 1,950 fps without expecting significant (read: bone rattling) recoil in return.

Terminal Medicine Formula:

$$T.Rx= \frac{ME+(BWx3.75)+(BDx1500)+(BIZx1.282x((BD/2)x(BD/2)x3.14)x2500))}{100+(SPI/900)+(PI/100)}$$

-or-

$$T.Rx=(ME+(BWx3.75)+(BDx1500)+(BIZx1.282x((BD/2)x(BD/2)x3.14)x2500))/100 +(SPI/900)+(PI/100)$$

where:
- ME = Muzzle Energy [=BSxBSx(BW/7000)/64.32]
- BW = Bullet Weight [grains: 1 grain = 1/7000th of a pound]
- BD = Bullet Diameter [inches]
- BIZ = Bullet Impact Zone value [as described above]
- PI = Penetration Index [=ME/((BD/2)x(BD/2)x3.14159)xSD]
- BS = Bullet Speed [feet per second]
- SD = Sectional Density [=BW/7000/(BDxBD)]
- SPI = Stopping Power Index [=(½BDx½BD)x3.14159xME]

Part 4: Tables & Errata

Table 1: rexGun Cartridges								
Cartridge	BD	BW	BS	ME	BIZ	SD	SPI	PI	T.Rx
4-bore Nitro (Modern Smokeless: FMJ Solid)	1.035	2,200	1,950	18,580	2.226	0.293	15,632	65	**362**
700 Hubel Express	.700	1,000	3,000	19,989	1.505	0.292	7,693	151	**277**
700 Nitro Express (Max Load)	.700	1,000	2,440	13,223	1.505	0.292	5,089	100	**205**
700 JDJ	.700	1,000	2,330	12,058	1.505	0.292	4,640	91	**193**
620 Gladney (& 600 OK)	.620	900	2,400	11,514	1.700	0.334	3,476	128	**180**
600 Nitro Express (Max Load- Bolt Action)	.620	900	2,300	10,574	1.700	0.334	3,192	117	**170**
577 Tyrannosaur (Max Load / & 14.5 JDJ)	.585	750	2,600	11,261	1.258	0.313	3,027	131	**165**
700/577 Nitro Express	.585	900	2,300	10,574	1.258	0.376	2,842	148	**164**
700 Holland & Holland	.700	1,000	2,000	8,884	1.505	0.292	3,419	67	**160**
585 Nyati (Max Load)	.585	750	2,530	10,662	1.258	0.313	2,866	124	**159**
577 Tyrannosaur (A-square)	.585	750	2,400	9,595	1.277	0.313	2,579	112	**148**
585 Gladney (& 577 Tyrannosaur)	.585	750	2,400	9,595	1.258	0.313	2,579	112	**148**
600 Nitro Express (Heavy Double Load)	.620	900	2,050	8,401	1.700	0.334	2,536	93	**147**
4-bore (B.P. Heavy Load: Lead / -40% TRx)	1.035	2,000	1,300	7,507	2.226	0.267	6,316	24	**140**
600 Nitro Express (Standard Load)	.620	900	1,950	7,601	1.700	0.334	2,295	84	**139**
50 BMG (Hand Load/ 18" bbl, repeater)	.510	600	2,700	9,715	1.097	0.330	1,985	157	**138**
775 Express Rigby (10-bore Nitro/Solid)	.775	1,100	1,500	5,497	1.667	0.262	2593	30	**136**
585 Gehringer	.585	750	2,250	8,433	1.258	0.313	2,267	98	**136**
475 LTD (Lott Tanner Dinosaur)	.475	500	3,000	9,995	1.022	0.317	1.771	179	**135**
475 Atkinson & Marquart Magnum	.475	500	2,980	9,862	1.022	0.317	1,748	176	**134**
585 Nyati (Common Load)	.585	750	2,200	8,062	1.258	0.313	2,167	94	**132**
600 Nitro Express (Tropical Load)	.620	900	1,850	6,841	1.700	0.334	2,065	76	**131**
"4-bore" (B.P. Common Lead Bullet/ -40% TRx)	.975	1,882	1,330	7,394	2.097	0.283	5,520	28	**129**

BD: Bore Diameter / BW: Bullet Weight / BS: Bullet Speed / ME: Muzzle Energy /
SD: Sectional Density / SPI: Shock Power Index / PI: Penetration Index /
BIZ: Bullet Impact Zone value: unless noted, BIZ values are based on Woodleigh Solids

| Table 1: rexGun Cartridges continued... | | | | | | | | | |
Cartridge	BD	BW	BS	ME	BIZ	SD	SPI	PI	T.Rx
600/577 Rewa	.585	750	2,150	7,700	1.258	0.313	2,070	90	**128**
600/577 JDJ	.620	900	1,800	6,477	1.700	0.334	1,955	72	**127**
730 Nitro Express (12-bore Nitro / FMJ)	.730	750	1,950	6,334	1.570	0.201	2,651	30	**127**
500 A-square (A-square Load)	.510	600	2,470	8,130	1.116	0.330	1,661	131	**122**
577 Nitro Express 3"	.585	750	2,050	7,000	1.258	0.313	1,882	82	**121**
510 Wells	.510	600	2,400	7,676	1.097	0.330	1,568	124	**117**
"4-bore" (B.P. Lead Ball / -40% TRx)	.975	1,400	1,500	6,996	2.097	0.210	5,224	20	**116**
500 Rafiki	.510	570	2,420	7,414	1.097	0.313	1,515	114	**113**
460 Weatherby (Barnes Mono-Solid FP)	.458	500	2,600	7,507	1.690	0.341	1,237	155	**113**
495 A-Square (A-square)	.510	570	2,400	7,292	1.114	0.313	1,490	112	**112**
460 Weatherby	.458	500	2,600	7,507	0.985	0.341	1,237	155	**109**
500 AHR	.510	570	2,350	6,991	1.097	0.313	1,428	107	**109**
12.5x70mm Schuler (& 500 Jeffery, Alt.)	.510	535	2,400	6,844	1.097	0.294	1,398	98	**106**
500 Jeffery (Rimless Jeffery)	.510	570	2,300	6,697	1.097	0.313	1,368	103	**106**
450 Vincent Long	.458	500	2,550	7,221	0.936	0.341	1,190	149	**106**
470 Mbogo	.475	500	2,500	6,941	1.022	0.317	1,230	124	**104**
475 Ackley Magnum (& 475 OKH Magnum)	.475	600	2,200	6,450	1.022	0.380	1,154	120	**103**
470 Capstick (Barnes Mono-Solid FP)	.475	500	2,400	6,397	1.753	0.317	1,134	114	**102**
577 Nitro Express 2¾"	.585	650	1,950	5,490	1.258	.271	1,476	105	**101**
470 Capstick (Sledgehammer)	.475	500	2,400	6,397	1.514	0.317	1,134	114	**101**
450 Dakota	.458	500	2,450	6,666	0.985	0.341	1,098	138	**100**
450 Ackley Mag. (Barnes Mono-Solid FP)	.458	500	2,380	6,290	1.690	0.341	1,036	130	**100**
450 Vincent Short	.458	500	2,440	6,612	0.985	0.341	1,089	137	**100**
460 A-square Short	.458	500	2,420	6,504	1.000	0.341	1,071	134	**98**
505 Gibbs	.505	525	2,300	6,168	1.086	0.294	1,236	91	**98**
470 Capstick (A-square)	.475	500	2,400	6,397	1.037	0.317	1,134	114	**98**
"8-bore" (B.P. Heavy Load: Lead / -40% TRx)	.875	1,250	1,500	6,247	1.882	0.233	3,756	24	**98**
500 Nitro Express 3"	.510	570	2,150	5,852	1.097	0.313	1,195	90	**97**

BD: Bore Diameter / BW: Bullet Weight / BS: Bullet Speed / ME: Muzzle Energy /
SD: Sectional Density / SPI: Shock Power Index / PI: Penetration Index /
BIZ: Bullet Impact Zone value: unless noted, BIZ values are based on Woodleigh Solids

Table 1: rexGun Cartridges continued...									
Cartridge	BD	BW	BS	ME	BIZ	SD	SPI	PI	T.Rx
450 Assegai (A-square)	.458	500	2,400	6,397	1.000	0.341	1,054	132	97
450 Watts (Barnes Mono-Solid FP)	.458	500	2,330	6,029	1.690	0.341	993	125	97
475 T&T Belted Rimless Magnum	.475	600	2,100	6,018	1.022	0.380	1,041	126	97
470 Royal	.475	500	2,370	6,238	1.022	0.317	1,105	111	96
450 Ackley Magnum	.458	500	2,380	6,290	0.985	0.341	1,036	130	96
505 Gibbs (22" bbl / Taylor's Ultimate DGR)	.505	525	2,260	5,956	1.086	0.294	1,193	87	96
450 Watts	.458	550	2,230	6,075	0.985	0.375	1,001	138	96
476 T&T Belted Rimless Magnum	.476	520	2,300	6,110	1.024	0.328	1,087	113	96
458 Lott (Barnes Monolithic Flat Point)	.458	500	2,300	5,875	1.690	0.341	968	121	96
500 Nitro Express 3¼"	.510	570	2,125	5,717	1.097	0.313	1,168	88	96
510 Nitro Express	.510	600	2,050	5,600	1.097	0.330	1,144	90	96
458 Canadian Magnum	.458	500	2,360	6,185	0.985	0.341	1,019	128	95
10.57 Meteor	.416	400	2,750	6,719	0.895	0.330	913	163	95
450 G&A Special	.458	500	2,350	6,133	0.985	0.341	1,010	127	95
458 Lott (Sledgehammer)	.458	500	2,300	5,875	1.460	0.341	968	121	94
458 Lott	.458	550	2,200	5,912	0.985	0.375	974	134	94
450 Watts	.458	500	2,330	6,029	0.985	0.341	993	125	93
476 T&T Belted Rimless Magnum	.476	480	2,370	5,988	1.024	0.303	1,066	102	93
465 Holland & Holland (Belted Magnum)	.468	480	2,375	6,013	1.007	0.313	1,034	109	93
475 T&T Belted Rimless Magnum	.475	500	2,300	5,875	1.022	0.317	1,041	105	93
416 Weatherby	.416	400	2,700	6,477	0.895	0.330	880	157	92
458 Lott (Barnes Monolithic Flat Point)	.458	450	2,400	5,757	1.690	0.306	948	107	92
459 Hedrat	.458	480	2,370	5,988	0.985	0.327	987	119	92
14.5mm Whisper	.585	750	1,600	4,264	1.258	0.313	1,146	50	92
458 Lott (& 458 KNR)	.458	500	2,300	5,875	0.985	0.341	968	121	92
470 Nitro Express (Barnes Monolithic F.P.)	.474	500	2,200	5,375	1.751	0.318	948	97	92
458 Lott	.458	550	2,150	5,647	0.985	0.375	930	128	91
450 Ackley Magnum (A-square)	.458	465	2,400	5,949	1.000	0.317	980	114	91
450 Rigby (Modern Rimless)	.458	480	2,350	5,888	0.985	0.327	970	117	91

BD: Bore Diameter / BW: Bullet Weight / BS: Bullet Speed / ME: Muzzle Energy /
SD: Sectional Density / SPI: Shock Power Index / PI: Penetration Index /
BIZ: Bullet Impact Zone value: unless noted, BIZ values are based on Woodleigh Solids

Table 1: rexGun Cartridges continued...									
Cartridge	BD	BW	BS	ME	BIZ	SD	SPI	PI	T.Rx
458 Lott (A-square)	.458	465	2,380	5,850	1.000	0.317	964	112	**90**
470 Nitro Express (Barnes Monolithic F.P.)	.474	500	2,150	5,133	1.751	0.318	906	92	**89**
476 Westley Richards Nitro Express	.476	520	2,150	5,339	1.024	0.328	950	98	**88**
470 Nitro Express (Sledgehammer)	.474	500	2,150	5,133	1.511	0.318	906	92	**88**
470 Nitro Express (W.R., 26" barrels)	.474	500	2,200	5,375	1.019	0.318	948	97	**87**
458 Lott (Lott's Perfect Elephant load)	.458	500	2,200	5375	0.985	0.341	886	111	**87**
450 Howell	.458	500	2,180	5,278	0.985	0.341	869	109	**86**
475 No.2 Jeffery Nitro Express	.488	500	2,150	5,133	1.050	0.300	960	82	**86**
476 Westley Richards Nitro Express	.476	520	2,100	5,093	1.024	0.328	906	94	**85**
470 Nitro Express (A-square)	.475	500	2,150	5,133	1.035	0.318	906	92	**85**
470 Nitro Express	.474	500	2,150	5,133	1.019	0.318	906	92	**85**
577 Express 2¾"	.585	650	1,650	3,930	1.258	0.271	1056	40	**85**
475 No.2 Nitro Express	.483	480	2,200	5,160	1.039	0.294	945	83	**85**
458 Win.Mag. (Original Intended Load)	.458	500	2,150	5,133	0.985	0.341	846	106	**84**
475 Nitro Express	.483	500	2,125	5,015	1.039	0.306	919	84	**84**
475 Nitro Express	.483	480	2,175	5,043	1.039	0.294	924	81	**84**
8-bore (B.P. Brass, Lead Ball / -40% TRx)	.875	875	1,650	5,291	1.882	0.163	3,182	14	**83**
475 Nitro Express	.476	480	2,175	5,043	1.024	0.303	897	86	**83**
458 Win.Mag. (Modern Load-Hornady)	.458	500	2,130	5,038	0.993	0.341	830	104	**83**
450 No.2 Nitro Express 3½"	.458	480	2,175	5,043	0.985	0.327	831	100	**82**
500/450 3¼" Nitro Express	.458	480	2,175	5,043	0.985	0.327	831	100	**82**
458 Winchester Magnum (A-square Load)	.458	465	2,220	5,090	1.000	0.317	839	98	**82**
45-348 Winchester Improved	.458	500	2,110	4,944	0.985	0.341	815	102	**82**
475 HUD	.475	500	2,090	4,851	1.022	0.317	860	87	**82**
500/465 Nitro Express	.468	480	2,150	4,928	1.007	0.313	848	90	**82**
450 Nitro Express 3¼"	.458	480	2,150	4,928	0.985	0.327	812	98	**81**

BD: Bore Diameter / BW: Bullet Weight / BS: Bullet Speed / ME: Muzzle Energy /
SD: Sectional Density / SPI: Shock Power Index / PI: Penetration Index /
BIZ: Bullet Impact Zone value: unless noted, BIZ values are based on Woodleigh Solids

Table 1: rexGun Cartridges continued...									
Cartridge	BD	BW	BS	ME	BIZ	SD	SPI	PI	T.Rx
416 Rigby (Barnes Mono-Solid FP)	.416	400	2,400	5,117	1.535	0.330	696	124	81
8-bore (B.P. Brass Lead Ball/ -40% TRx)	.835	875	1,650	5,291	1.796	0.179	2897	17	80
458 Win.Mag. (Modern Improved Load)	.458	500	2,040	4,622	0.985	0.341	761	96	79
416 Rigby	.416	410	2,370	5,115	0.895	0.338	695	127	79
425 Express	.423	400	2,400	5,117	0.910	0.319	719	116	79
425 Westley Richards	.435	410	2,350	5,029	0.936	0.310	747	105	79
416 Rigby (A-square)	.416	400	2,400	5,117	0.908	0.330	696	124	78
416 Hoffman (& 10.75 Maverick)	.416	400	2,400	5,117	0.895	0.330	696	124	78
416 Remington Magnum (& 416 Rimmed)	.416	400	2,400	5,117	0.895	0.330	696	124	78
411 Magnum (& 411 K.D.F.)	.411	400	2,400	5,117	0.884	0.338	679	130	78
400 Pondoro (A-square)	.409	400	2,400	5,117	0.893	0.342	672	133	78
378 Weatherby	.375	300	2,900	5,604	0.806	0.305	619	155	78
400 Holland & Holland	.411	400	2,375	5,011	0.884	0.338	665	128	77
500/416 Nitro Express 3¼"	.416	410	2,330	4,944	0.895	0.338	672	123	77
450 Fuller (& 450 Alaskan)	.458	500	2,000	4,442	0.985	0.341	732	92	77
8-bore (B.P. Paper, Lead Ball / -40% TRx)	.835	875	1,575	4,821	1.796	0.179	2,640	16	77
450 Rigby's "Special" Rifle for Big Game	.458	480	2,050	4,480	0.985	0.327	738	89	77
416 Taylor	.416	400	2,350	4,906	0.895	0.330	667	119	76
458 Winchester Magnum (Common Load)	.458	500	1,950	4,223	0.985	0.341	696	87	75
404 Jeffrey (Improved Load)	.423	400	2,300	4,700	0.910	0.319	660	107	74
375 Remington Ultra Magnum	.375	300	2,760	5,039	0.806	0.305	557	139	72
10-bore (B.P. Common Lead Bullet / -40% TRx)	.775	875	1,550	4,669	1.667	0.208	2,203	21	71
404 Jeffrey (Original Load)	.423	400	2,200	4,300	0.910	0.319	604	98	70
375 Holland & Holland 350-gr	.375	350	2,400	4,478	0.806	0.356	495	144	68
416 Aagard	.416	400	2,160	4,145	0.895	0.330	563	101	68
411 Express & Hawk	.411	400	2,160	4,145	0.884	0.338	550	106	68
450/400 Nitro Express 3¼"	.411	400	2,150	4,107	0.884	0.338	545	105	68

BD: Bore Diameter / BW: Bullet Weight / BS: Bullet Speed / ME: Muzzle Energy /
SD: Sectional Density / SPI: Shock Power Index / PI: Penetration Index /
BIZ: Bullet Impact Zone value: unless noted, BIZ values are based on Woodleigh Solids

Cartridge	BD	BW	BS	ME	BIZ	SD	SPI	PI	T.Rx
416 Barnes	.416	400	2,140	4,069	0.895	0.330	553	99	67
404 Jeffrey (Original Load)	.423	400	2,125	4,012	0.910	0.319	564	91	67
450/400 Nitro Express 3"	.408	400	2,125	4,012	0.877	0.343	524	105	67
9.3x64 Brenneke	.366	286	2,650	4,461	0.787	0.305	469	129	65
9.5x73 Miller-Greiss Magnum	.375	271	2,670	4,291	0.066	0.275	474	107	63
10-bore (B.P. Rifle Load: Lead / -40% TRx)	.775	700	1,600	3,980	1.667	0.166	1878	14	63
375 Holland & Holland Belted Magnum	.375	300	2,500	4,164	0.806	0.305	460	115	63
12-bore (Heavy Load: Lead / -40% TRx)	.730	750	1,550	4,002	1.570	0.201	1,675	19	61
375 H&H Flanged Magnum	.375	300	2,400	3,838	0.806	0.305	424	106	60
400/350 Nitro Express (W.R. Modern Load)	.358	310	2,350	3,802	0.770	0.346	383	131	59
45-70 Magnum	.458	500	1,525	2,583	0.985	0.341	425	53	58
369 Nitro Express (Purdey)	.375	270	2,500	3,748	0.806	0.274	414	93	57
360 No.2 Nitro Express	.366	320	2,200	3,440	0.787	0.339	364	110	56
9.3x62 Mauser (& 9.3x74R, Improved Loads)	.366	286	2,360	3,538	0.787	0.305	372	103	56
10-bore (Lt. Paradox Load: Lead / -40% TRx)	.775	700	1,300	2,627	1.667	0.166	1239	9	54
9.3x74R (Original Heavy Load)	.366	293	2,280	3,383	0.787	0.312	356	100	54
12-bore (*Explora* Load: Lead / -40% TRx)	.730	735	1,300	2,759	1.570	0.197	1155	13	53
9.3x74R (Original Load)	.366	285	2,280	3,291	0.787	0.304	346	95	53
12-bore (Rifle Load: Lead Ball / -40% TRx)	.730	580	1,600	3,298	1.570	0.155	1380	12	53
400/375 Belted Nitro Express (H&H)	.375	320	2,075	3,060	0.806	0.325	338	90	52
333 Jeffery Rimless	.333	300	2,200	3,225	0.716	0.386	281	143	52
500 B.P.E. (Hardened Lead/ -20% TRx)	.510	480	1,700	3,081	1.097	0.264	629	40	52
400/350 Rigby	.358	310	2,150	3,183	0.770	0.346	320	109	51
300 Winchester Magnum	.308	220	2,680	3,510	0.662	0.331	261	156	51
333 Jeffery Flanged	.333	300	2,150	3,080	0.716	0.386	268	137	51
350 Rigby No.2	.358	225	2,575	3,314	0.770	0.251	334	83	50

BD: Bore Diameter / BW: Bullet Weight / BS: Bullet Speed / ME: Muzzle Energy /
SD: Sectional Density / SPI: Shock Power Index / PI: Penetration Index /
BIZ: Bullet Impact Zone value: unless noted, BIZ values are based on Woodleigh Solids

Table 1: rexGun Cartridges continued...									
Cartridge	BD	BW	BS	ME	BIZ	SD	SPI	PI	T.Rx
500 Nitro for Black (Hard. Lead/ -20% TRx)	.510	400	1,900	3,207	1.097	0.220	655	34	**50**
450 Nitro for Black (Hard. Lead/ -20% TRx)	.458	365	2,100	3,575	0.985	0.249	589	54	**50**
9.3x62 Mauser (Original Load)	.366	285	2,175	2,994	0.787	0.304	315	87	**50**
450 Express (Selous' Cart. / Hard. Lead -20%)	.461	540	1,550	2,881	0.991	0.363	481	63	**50**
450/400 Nitro Express 2&3/8"	.407	400	1,650	2,419	0.875	0.345	315	64	**50**
318 Westley Richards (Rimless Nitro Exp.)	.330	250	2,400	3,198	0.710	0.328	274	123	**50**
12-bore (B.P. Pardox / Lead Ball -40% T.Rx)	.730	580	1,300	2,177	1.570	0.155	911	8	**46**
30-06 Springfield	.308	220	2,410	2,838	0.662	0.331	211	126	**44**
308 Winchester	.308	220	2,320	2,630	0.662	0.331	196	117	**42**
450 B.P.E. (Hardened Lead/ -20% TRx)	.458	365	1,700	2,343	0.985	0.249	386	35	**40**
8x57 Mauser	.333	226	2,100	2,214	0.716	0.291	193	74	**39**
450 Express (B.P. Selous' Lion Load- Lead -30%)	.461	360	1910	2917	0.991	0.242	447	42	**39**
303 British	.312	215	2,060	2,026	0.671	0.316	155	84	**36**
275 Rigby (7x57 Mauser)	.284	173	2,300	2,033	0.611	0.306	129	98	**33**
450 Express (B.P. Min. Red Deer Load- Lead) -30%	.461	310	1,800	2,231	0.991	0.208	372	28	**33**
243 Winchester	.243	100	2,960	1,946	0.523	0.242	90	102	**29**
223 Remington	.223	60	3,100	1,281	0.480	0.172	50	57	**20**

BD: Bore Diameter / BW: Bullet Weight / BS: Bullet Speed / ME: Muzzle Energy /
SD: Sectional Density / SPI: Shock Power Index / PI: Penetration Index /
BIZ: Bullet Impact Zone value: unless noted, BIZ values are based on Woodleigh Solids

Table 2: Species Specific T.Rx Values

Tyrannosaurus rex T.Rx

Game Class	Min	Adq	Pro	Imp	Sup	Stop
sub-adult *T. rex* (4.5 tons)	69	78	87	96	105	114
small adult *T. rex* (6 tons)	72	81	90	99	108	117
common adult *T. rex* (9 tons)	75	84	93	102	111	120
large adult *T. rex* (12 tons)	78	87	96	105	114	123
record-size *T. rex* (18 tons)	81	90	99	108	117	126

African elephant T.Rx

Game Class	Min	Adq	Pro	Imp	Sup	Stop
sub-adult - bush (3 tons)	53	62	71	80	89	98
small adult - bush (4.5 tons)	56	65	74	83	92	101
common adult - bush (6 tons)	59	68	77	86	95	104
large adult - bush (9 tons)	62	71	80	89	98	107
record-size - bush (12 tons)	65	74	83	92	101	110

T.Rx values indicated are accurate to within +/- one (1) point margin of error
Min= Minimum / Adq= Adequate / Pro= Proper /
Imp= Improved / Sup= Superior / Stop= Stopping

Table 3: Terminal Effectiveness Comparison								
Tyrannosaurus rex vs. African elephant								
Cartridge	BD	BW	BS	ME	BIZ	SD	SPI	PI	T.Rx
For T.rex...									
500 Jeffery	.510	535	2,400	6,844	1.097	0.294	1,398	98	**106**
...as for Elephant									
458 Lott (A-square)	.458	465	2,380	5,850	1.000	0.317	964	112	**90**
For T.rex...									
500 Nitro Express 3"	.510	570	2,150	5,852	1.097	0.313	1,195	90	**97**
...as for Elephant									
450 Nitro Express 3¼"	.458	480	2,150	4,928	0.985	0.327	812	98	**81**
For T.rex...									
465 H&H (Belted Magnum)	.468	480	2,375	6,013	1.007	0.313	1,034	109	**93**
...as for Elephant									
400 Holland & Holland	.411	400	2,375	5,011	0.884	0.338	665	128	**77**
For T.rex...									
475 Nitro Express	.483	500	2,125	5,015	1.039	0.306	919	84	**84**
...as for Elephant									
450/400 Nitro Express 3¼"	.411	400	2,150	4,107	0.884	0.338	545	105	**68**
For T.rex...									
416 Rigby	.416	410	2,370	5,115	0.895	0.338	695	127	**79**
...as for Elephant									
375 H&H Belted Magnum	.375	300	2,500	4,164	0.806	0.305	460	115	**63**
For T.rex...									
450/400 Nitro Express 3"	.408	400	2,125	4,012	0.877	0.343	524	105	**67**
...as for Elephant									
400/350 Rigby	.358	310	2,150	3,183	0.770	0.346	320	109	**51**
For T.rex...									
375 H&H Flanged Magnum	.375	300	2,400	3,838	0.806	0.305	424	106	**60**
...as for Elephant									
30-06 Springfield	.308	220	2,410	2,838	0.662	0.331	211	126	**44**

BD: Bore Diameter / BW: Bullet Weight / BS: Bullet Speed / ME: Muzzle Energy /
SD: Sectional Density / SPI: Shock Power Index / PI: Penetration Index /
BIZ: Bullet Impact Zone value: unless noted, BIZ values are based on Woodleigh Solids
T.Rx: Terminal Medicine values based on A.E. to T.rex adjustment of 16pts (+/-1)

Table 4: Weight to T.Rx

Game T.Rx (examples: elephant, rhino, african/asiatic buffalo, hippo, giraffe, deer, gazelle, etc.)

Predator T.Rx (examples: T. rex, lion, leopard, etc. and following up wounded elephant & a/a buffalo)

Tonnage	Minimum	Adequate	Proper	Improved	Superior	Stopping	Weight
0.047	17 / 30	26 / 39	35 / 48	44 / 57	53 / 66	62 / 75	94 lbs
0.07	20 / 33	29 / 42	38 / 51	47 / 60	56 / 69	65 / 78	140
0.094	23 / 36	32 / 45	41 / 54	50 / 63	59 / 72	68 / 81	188
0.14	26 / 39	35 / 48	44 / 57	53 / 66	62 / 75	71 / 84	280
0.1875	29 / 42	38 / 51	47 / 60	56 / 69	65 / 78	74 / 87	375
0.281	32 / 45	41 / 54	50 / 63	59 / 72	68 / 81	77 / 90	562
0.375	35 / 48	44 / 57	53 / 66	62 / 75	71 / 84	80 / 93	750
0.5625	38 / 51	47 / 60	56 / 69	65 / 78	74 / 87	83 / 96	1,125
0.75	41 / 54	50 / 63	59 / 72	68 / 81	77 / 90	86 / 99	1,500
1.125	44 / 57	53 / 66	62 / 75	71 / 84	80 / 93	89 / 102	2,250
1.5	47 / 60	56 / 69	65 / 78	74 / 87	83 / 96	92 / 105	3,000
2.25	50 / 63	59 / 72	68 / 81	77 / 90	86 / 99	95 / 108	4,500
3	53 / 66	62 / 75	71 / 84	80 / 93	89 / 102	98 / 111	6,000
4.5	56 / 69	65 / 78	74 / 87	83 / 96	92 / 105	101 / 114	9,000
6	59 / 72	68 / 81	77 / 90	86 / 99	95 / 108	104 / 117	12,000
9	62 / 75	71 / 84	80 / 93	89 / 102	98 / 111	107 / 120	18,000
12	65 / 78	74 / 87	83 / 96	92 / 105	101 / 114	110 / 123	24,000
18	68 / 81	77 / 90	86 / 99	95 / 108	104 / 117	113 / 126	36,000
24	71 / 84	80 / 93	89 / 102	98 / 111	107 / 120	116 / 129	48,000

T.Rx values indicated are accurate to within a +/- two (2) points margin of error.

This T. rex is more accurate than most images, in terms of stance, posture, and bulk.

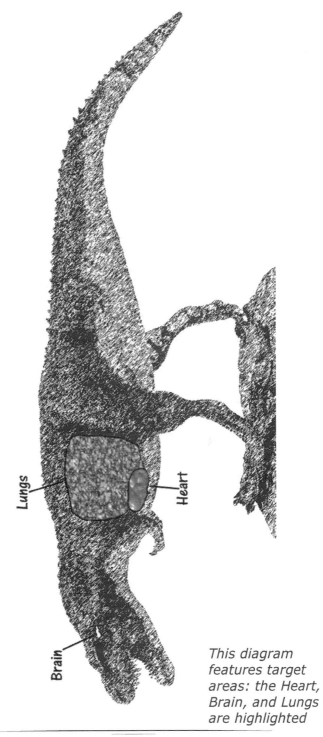

Lungs

Heart

Brain

This diagram features target areas: the Heart, Brain, and Lungs are highlighted

BIBLIOGRAPHY

Adam, R. *The World's Most Powerful Rifles and Handguns.* Secaucus, New Jersey: Chartwell Books, 1991

Akehurst, R. *Game Guns & Rifles – Percussion to Hammerless Ejector in Britain,* Trowbridge, Wiltshire, GB: The Sportsman's Press, 1996

Alphin, A.B. *Any Shot You Want – The A-Square Handloading and Rifle Manual,* Bedford, KY: On Target Press, 1996

Austyn, C. *Classic Sporting Rifles,* Long Beach, CA: Safari Press, 1997

Barnes, F.C. *Cartridges of the World, 8th edition,* Northbrook, IL: DBI Books, 1997

Benton, Dr. M. *The Dinosaur Encyclopedia – A Handbook for Dinosaur Enthusiasts of All Ages!,* New York: Simon and Schuster, 1984

Boddington, C. *Safari Rifles,* Long Beach, CA: Safari Press, 1990

Capstick, F.C. *The Diana Files – The Huntress-Traveller Through History,* Houghton, South Africa: Rowland Ward Publications, 2004

Capstick, P.H. *Death in the Dark Continent,* New York: St. Martin's Press, 1983

Capstick, P.H. *Death in the Long Grass,* New York: St. Martin's Press, 1977

Capstick, P.H. *Maneaters* Long Beach, CA: Safari Press, 1981

Capstick, P.H. *Safari – The Last Adventure,* New York: St. Martin's Press, 1984

Carmichel, J. *Book of the Rifle,* New York: Outdoor Life Books, 1985

Currie, P.J. and Padian, K. *Encyclopedia of Dinosaurs,* San Diego, CA: Academic Press, 1997

De Camp, L.S. *A Gun for Dinosaur,* Garden City, NY: Doubleday & Company, Inc., 1963

Fadala, S. *Rifle Guide,* South Hackensack, NJ: Stoeger Publishing Company, 1993

George, J.N. *English Guns and Rifles,* Plantersville, SC: Small-Arms Technical Publishing Company, 1947

Greener, W.W. *The Gun and its Development,* London: Cassell And Company, Ltd., 1910

Lott, J. *Big Bore Rifles,* Los Angeles, CA: Peterson Publishing Company, 1983

Hayes, T. *The Modern Hunting Rifle,* South Brunswick, NJ: A.S. Barnes and Company, 1966

Herne, B. *White Hunters – The Golden Age of African Safaris,* New York: Henry Holt and Company, 1999

Keith, E. *Guns & Ammo for Hunting Big Game,* Los Angeles, CA: Peterson Publishing Company, 1965

Klups, N. *Double Barrel,* Atlen, PA: Schiffer Military History, 2007

Ness, F.C. *Practical Dope on Big Bores,* Prescott, AZ: Wolfe Publishing Company, 1984

Patterson, Lt. Col. J.H. *The Man-eaters of Tsavo,* New York: St. Martin's Press, 1986

Paul, G.S. *The Scientific American book of Dinosaurs – The Best Minds in Paleontology Create a Portrait of the Prehistoric Era,* New York: St. Martin's Press, 2000

Paul, G.S. *Predatory Dinosaurs of the World – A Complete Illustrated Guide,* New York: Simon and Schuster, 1988

Prothero, W. *Safari: A Dangerous Affair,* Long Beach, CA: Safari Press, 2000

Sloan, C. *Supercroc – and the Origin of Crocodiles,* Washington, D.C.: National Geographic, 2002

Taylor, J. *African Rifles & Cartridges,* Georgetown, SC: Small Arms Technical Publishing Company, 1948

Taylor, J. *Maneaters and Marauders,* Long Beach, CA: Safari Press, 2005

Truesdell, S.R. *the Rifle – Its Development for Big-Game Hunting,* Long Beach, CA: Safari Press, 1992

Waterman, C.F. *The Treasury of Sporting Guns,* New York: Random House, 1979

Wieland, T. *Dangerous-Game Rifles,* Camden, ME: Countrysport Press, 2006

Woods, G. *Rifles for Africa,* Long Beach, CA: Safari Press, 2002

The author shooting his Ferlach .470 N.E. Double Rifle

About the Author

Dr. Stephen W. Templar has worked in Law Enforcement, Corrections, Corporate Security Management and in several other professional, technical and high-security environments. He has extensive experience with all types of firearms, both at work and for sport. He is a collector of art and antiques, though none of his interests compares to his passion for firearms and their uses.

11437056R0006

Made in the USA
Lexington, KY
04 October 2011